VIOLETS

Chelsea Connor

India | USA | UK

Presentation by *BookLeaf Publishing*

Web: www.bookleafpub.com

E-mail: info@bookleafpub.com

ISBN: 9789358315431

First edition 2023

Max & Kitt

I love you eternally, without condition.

ACKNOWLEDGEMENT

To BookLeaf Publishing for giving me the opportunity to release this, it's truly something i can scratch off the bucket list, and i couldn't be more grateful for the chance.

To my sons, Max and Kitt, my reason for being. Thank you for showing me a love i didn't know existed, you will forever be the most important and precious part of my life. You are both my heart.

To my family, my Nan for your consistent love, to my Grandad for being the only man i could ever truly rely on, to Jennie, for never giving up your love for me. And to the rest of my family, my adoration for you is never wavering and each of you have supported and shaped me in your own ways.

To my friends who have been there for me even in the real thick of it, Nat and Demi, for your solid support and your love, my soul sisters. And Beth, for being the most non-judgmental space i could sit in.

To Grace Hetherington and Caroline
Saffron-Cherry, the two woman who believed
me and have stayed with me for years, you
spurred me on many times which pushed me to
produce scripts i'll forever be proud of, but i
wouldn't of gotten anywhere in this ruthless field
if you hadn't of opened the door and joined the
journey, and being the most compassionate
women possible.

& to The Thread. Once in a lifetime.

PREFACE

I wrote this collection of poems within a short
burst after a painful few years, the words were
bursting at the seams, apparently. Every word in
every line is brutally and sometimes painfully
honest, but laying my heart open on every page
has helped me more than any other form of
therapy every would. We all have our way of
swimming back, 'Violets' turned out to be mine.

This is written for the chronic people-pleasers.
The 'burdens'. The lost. The one's who feel like
everything should of fell together by now,
surely. The doubtful. The 'winging it'. The ones
who struggle to navigate the complexity of being
here.

Sometimes it's not true. The mind can be
crippling and negative at times. You're not a
burden. You're doing okay.

Take your time to heal.

Facade

If this feeling
is truly one you've never felt before
how can you look into my sore eyes
and tell me you don't want it anymore?

A painful regression
If I could go back and meet her
I'd show her compassion
Id talk with her, about the way she's acting
And call her out on the search for flirtatious
validation

Just as she is
I want to tell her she's enough
And dig her out of the cluster of self-deprecating
jokes
Poor attempt at a cover up

I'd give her a space where she doesn't have to be
performative
Just let her feel and sit with it
I'd tell her that she's wonderful, remind her to
not be so insecure
Talk more, talk until your voice gets hoarse

I'd wonder what she's looking for with the
consistent home hopping
And that it's okay to be selfish at times
I'd remind her that she's loved
I'd ask her not to leave herself behind

'Violet is pretty..'

Sunflower yellow dress

Tounge taste test

Inhale another ivory line

They thought we we're moving too quickly

That child of mine

Decided not to stay

Tranexamic acid, three times a day.

A Full Heart

Staring into eyes the same shade as mine
A lifeline I cling to like a raft in the vast
Your smile is Christmas Eve
Your first laugh was the eighth wonder
As I felt you absorb
As I felt you grow
I changed into a women barely even know

Know that where ever you go
Down the darkest of roads
Ill hold you as tightly as I do now
I'd fight until my last breath
My hand forever outstretched
To make sure you're doing your best

You made me stay
I gave you life, and you gave me the same
So remember this,
When I'm mad,
The first time smoke hits your lungs
If I'm overstimulated, lash my tounge
When we laugh until our eyes star to water
Just remember beautiful boy,
I'll always love you in lurid colour,

Break It Down

Go ahead and stress me out,
And I'll fly to the clouds.
A vessel still present, a shadow oozes poison
Trying to pull me back down to earth,
I'll bite like an abandoned dog, unaware of the
pain I'm causing

I'll set fire to the bar, and do nothing by
half-measure
Become everyone's 'last chance' stressor
Overstimulated by the pressure of validating
pleasure
Energized by the chance of a 'now or never'
endeavour
Fuck it off and give it up, it's been this way
forever.
'You've got to try and get it together'
'It'll be fine, you just need to get better.'

I chase my old thoughts like a stalker
A bursting heart, but still an unlovable daughter
Hand me a gift from god, and watch me tear it to
shreds
Filling up the space in my chest with pained
regrets

The fix is golden, unconditional love
The change I can't seem to find inbetween the
cushions of a strangers couch
So trace my spine, and lift the bottle to my
mouth

Let It Go

White sheets
Dried blood
But he touched my skin like nobody else would

What I wouldn't give,
To go back to camping under the sheets
Touching feet
Speaking a language nobody understood
Because we made it just for us

If you would of let me run home
I'd have raced until my feet turned black
You know I tried
And I tried
For that.

We was unaware of the cannibal waiting in the
shadows
With an appetite for a decade,
Spotted a broken bird
And crumbled two soulmates

You told me you hope I'd choke on the shame
So I swallow it like bad medicine
Everyday.

Fight Of The Flame

Are we all really strangers?
When we all feel the same?
Sonder fumes us together like February fog
But there's a flame you'll meet
Only once.

I knew it would hurt from the start, and I jumped
in
Willingly
With both feet
Two lips, one kiss
One house, two fists
Blonde hair, two kids
His shark eyes, had enough of this

After our passion turned to flames
We fell in too deep
But nothing could kill us,
There's nothing that strong
We had to face the music, but terrified of the
song

I was constantly putting my heart in danger
Just for bare minimum behaviour
You'd drag me down into the soil

Desperate, catching breath from inner turmoil
And I'd stay there,
Cause the sound of you packing your bags again,
I couldn't bare

I feel like everything's a test
Just to see how much you can cage me within
my head
Put I'd always pass, and with forgiveness I'd
prove it

Call me a star student
So when we've screamed words that have
bruised our hearts,
We always remember,
We both jumped in the fire
Forever charred.

So as always, I give you my heart,
You can kick it across the living room like a ball,
Or tear it apart with your bare hands like fresh
meat
And I'd dissociate and wait
Patiently, to see the man who I met in June
Sweet and kind, and cried laughing over drinks

I quietly accepted this life comes with chaotic
mess
I'm not scared of death

I'm not scared of loss
But i get a cold chill throughout my flesh
At the thought of being burnt by his flame.

Bend The Gender

I'd feel confident.
I'd never have to explain my theories

I'd be a bachelor.
King size bed like carousel of bodies

I'd be mysterious and play mind games,
It would be considered charming
I'd put my hand on women's thighs
Play it off as 'dis-arming'

I'd be rude to your face.
Then blame the silence on your poor humour
bone
I'd be bold and express my opinions
Without being told to watch to my tone

If I cheated,
It would mean I'm so unbelievably desired
If she does it,
She's messed in the head, wrongly wired.

If I told a joke,
I'd be the light of the room, hilarious.
When she quips back,

She's hiding behind something dark, oh so
precarious.
I'd turn the gas lights on
Until you smoother on the air
But when she did it
she broke your heart
oh so unfair

So Perfect

A freshly printed train ticket
If his promise of unconditional was true
Then his heart would still be in it

Cause betrayal can fall both ways
But he'll never feel as sorry as me
Shut the door of dialogue, petrified
accountability
Little happy family.

To The Max

The curl of your hair you'll find in my diluted
genes
Denim eyes, I love you like you'll never believe
I'll pull back the chord and open you up, so
you'll know you're free to speak
Two hearts are filled with love to bring you up
Trading cards and laughing hard, I wish my will
that it's enough

Equable, unapologetic bubble burst
That pressure lives in your stomach, dispirited
boy, you were my first
So we both know that will never be true
Whether It's butting heads or cuddles in bed,
you have to know something, the cadence, the
set stone
That my first true love my soul experienced in
this world
Will always
Be you.

Recovered

15

You don't have to hurt
I know I've met her before
Salvation exists.

Packet In

The first time I felt you, it was just like warm
honey
You found me at the weakest spot, and took
everything from me
Like a bailiff punching at the door, the floors
wooden bare but you begged for more
I gave you everything, my heart, my mind, dim
my spark to be a comatose darling
Flipped every feeling to the clouds, so you sat
on my back like an insatiable beast
I offered the grit scraps I had left of me, weak in
the heat, you impatiently snarled

My friends can drop you like a bad habit, forget
they even had it
Never discriminate who you bite, you had me
scanning strangers eyes in shopping queues
Turned myself into a ghost on repeat, and no one
ever pressed the issue, cause the aftermath is
messy like his dirty tissues
You're my best friend and my worst enemy, a
paradox I'll surrender to until I cross the stop
sign
But I don't feel nine foot tall tonight, so I'm
needing you one more time

When I decided to cut you off, I didn't believe
me either, so I don't blame them
But I daydreamed association and sound mind,
glossy counter tops and structured tea times
I was underneath the weight of it all like the
smallest Russian doll
There's no point in commiserating wasted time
Still sick with the agony of being sorry, except
now I hawk eye the mirror like arching pray

There she is. It's good to have you back.

Chestnut Boy

We ate the same dinner

Felt the same way

He just grew the other way He hit out

I hit in

He spat his pain out

Refusing to digest

I swallowed

Distressed.

That's why my heart beats out of my chest at
night

While his rises steady.

He brings me heat

He brings me peace

He pushes me out to sea

With a boat he made From Evergreen.

Helped to escape a fate

That wasn't meant to be.

All that time

He lived just a road away from me.

Glass Empty

Don't try to save him
Just another broken boy
You're more important

Bay

I held a soft spot for the Jason Bateman kinda
vibe

Unavailable.

Daddy Issues, suit and tie

I'd wait for something warm from his mouth

'More like a brother'

But I wore pink silk when we held each other.

I'd crack him open with devotion

Forgot the pledge, skipped to another.

Yours

Sweating my sins out

He shouldn't have had to

Cry in his mother's arms like a little boy

My heart never changed. It should never have
crashed to breaking point.

Hates harder every time I open the kitchen door

His ego paramount with broken eyes in tow

Crystal blue to a smudged dis-stain

Was it real?

I should never have believed so

'Forever and always.'

Now we sit and watch the rain smash the pave

Through different windows.

The Bad and the Good

Throw the bait to the sharks
Or slow down my car
Just to stutter to the strangers of the street
Salacious details of our depart
Desperate to find new faces to scream at

I'd rather lay myself than throw my loved under
the bus
But if you couldn't deflect easy in the arms of
Funny remarks
And was asked to pen the words
About how you truly feel
How would yours sound?

Dig through the wasteland and it's ugly
Dig through again and it's lovely.

Sun in Pink

Rose-coloured glasses
Only shade I'd want to see
Suited me perfect.